THE KIDS GUIDE TO SELLING

How I Was Able To Make $4,000 In 60 Days

Tanya Rogers
David Rogers

Rogers Publishing

Copyright © 2020 David Rogers

All rights reserved

Selling For Kids Book Series
Volume 1 - The Kids Guide To Selling: How I was Able To Make $4,000 in 60 Days
Volume 2 - The Teens Guide To Starting Your Own Business: Your Step by Step Blueprint to Becoming a Teen Entrepreneur
Volume 3 - The Teens Guide to Becoming an Entrepreneur: 102 Ways That You Can Start to Think Like a Successful Entrepreneur.
Volume 4 – The Teens Guide to Mastering Sales: How You Need to Think to Become Successful at Selling

No part of this book may be reproduced, or stored in a retrieval system, or transmitted in any form or by any means, electronic, mechanical, photocopying, recording, or otherwise, without express written permission of the publisher.

We can not guarantee that your results will be the same as the author's. This material is for educational purposes only.

Cover design by: David Rogers
Printed in the United States of America

CONTENTS

Title Page
Copyright
How to Get the Most From this Book
Introduction: Why I Wrote This Book
Chapter 1: Why You Need to Sell — 1
Chapter 2: Why Goals Are So Important — 7
Chapter 3: Attitude Is Key — 14
Chapter 4: What Product to Sell — 20
Chapter 5: Where and When to Sell — 26
Chapter 6: Pricing, Income, and Profit — 32
Chapter 7: How to Sell — 39
Chapter 8: Putting The Pieces Together — 46
Sign Up For The Selling For Kids Newsletter — 53
About The Author — 55
About The Author — 57
Books In This Series — 59
Follow Us — 61

HOW TO GET THE MOST FROM THIS BOOK

Step #1: Register Your Copy Of The Kids Guide To Selling For Free

When you register, you will get exclusive access to Advance Reader Copies of future releases, offers, discounts, plus tips and training.

Click Here to register or

Go to >> SellingForKids.com/Guide

Step #2: Read The Entire Book And Then Take Immediate Action

We created this book so that it can be read quickly and you can get started as soon as possible. Don't delay and get started on your journey today.

INTRODUCTION: WHY I WROTE THIS BOOK

After producing $4,000 in profit in just 60 days and realizing its impact on me, and what it could do for other people, I started to write this book.

My goal for this guide is to help young kids, teens, and adults to start selling and show you that it not only impacts how much money you'll have in your "piggy bank," but how it can affect your mind and your body as well.

In **The Kids Guide to Selling,** you will learn about the nine fundamental principles you need to know to start your own business. Plus, you will learn what you need to do Right Now to start selling and generating an income, following our simple and inexpensive business model.

We created the **Selling for Kids Book Series** because we want to teach a future generation of young entrepreneurs what they can do right now to begin their journey on the path of success.

CHAPTER 1: WHY YOU NEED TO SELL

"While school teaches you how to be a great employee, I'm going to teach you how to be a great entrepreneur."

-TANYA ROGERS

In this book, I will share the process I used to make $4,000 in 60 days. By the time you are done with this book, you will have all the knowledge to duplicate this process yourself and be well on your way to generating income anytime you want. The great thing about this process is that it can work for anyone at any age.

I have learned that there are nine main parts of this process; Goals, Attitude, Product, Where and When to Sell, Price, Income, Profit, and Practice. Over the next few chapters, we will be going into each of these parts in detail so that you can understand them and how they all work together.

Before we get started, I think it's important to tell you the story of how I got started so that you can see that you and I probably started at the same place.

My Journey Begins

The beginning of my journey in selling wasn't with the intention of selling. Like most schools, my school would have several fundraisers throughout the year, and my parents wanted to help. They would buy about $400-$500 worth of candy or items during each fundraiser. As I'm sure many others do, my school did not want the kids selling door to door or to strangers. So, the candy would usually just sit around the house until we eventually threw them away.

Neither my parents nor I knew what was possible with all those items we had spent our hard-earned money on buying. Around the time I turned 12 years old, we had an idea. How about we go ahead and resale the candy we had purchased from the school to make our money back? Typically, this is what you would be doing with fundraising candy from school. However, since our school did not allow this, we weren't doing this at the start. Once we started to do this, we were quickly able to make our money back.

That's when our thinking kicked up a notch. We started to think of these candy bars from the school as an investment in products or merchandise. If we paid one dollar for each bar, why not mark up the price a little bit. So, instead of selling them $1 and just making our money back, we sold them for $2 and made a dollar profit off of each one. This was the start of something beautiful.

What Selling Meant To Me

At the age of 12, I viewed selling as just a career that older adults took up to make money for their family, and it seemed unimportant to my life. Selling just seemed to distract me from the "unproductive tasks" I wanted to accomplish, such as finishing a tv show or playing video games. My first times selling were more of an obligation for me than a fun time. My attitude wasn't positive because I didn't want to sell; I wanted to binge-watch Netflix.

However, as I grew more mature into adolescence, I realized that selling was not just a career but a way of life. What exactly changed? Well, I made a goal of what I wanted to make money for, and then I achieved that goal. The realization for me, that if I work passionately towards a goal with a positive mindset, the results are much better for my family and me.

Selling soon became a way to have fun through goals, which I will discuss later in the next chapter. It came with an incentive most kids wanted, vacations. After all, what child wouldn't want a season pass to Universal Studios or a week-long vacation to Circus Circus Las Vegas? I set my goal, bought my merchandise, and worked out how much profit I would need to make for the vacation.

But selling for a vacation isn't the only fun thing that can happen. You can sell to buy a game. You can sell to buy a laptop. You can sell to buy your first car. Just about anything you can dream up, you can sell to achieve.

Who's This Book For?

This book isn't just for elementary students, middle schoolers, or high schoolers. This guide to selling is for people of all ages.

I also want to emphasize to parents who read this that selling is a great way to create a strong work ethic in a child's life. Just because I'm writing this in high school doesn't mean you need to start selling in high school. Start as soon as you can. It is essential to bring to a child's mind that money doesn't grow on trees and that parents aren't a personal bank account.

It is better for you as parents to teach your children the importance of creating an income stream at a young age, so they don't get surprised when they have to work in college or adult life. Not only will it help later in their work life, but now in their school life as well.

Won't I Fall Behind At School?

As a parent, you may worry that your child may fall behind in school. Well, you shouldn't have to worry too much. The more experience they get at selling, generally, the better they become at it and don't require as much time to do it. As an example, we'll look at my personal experiences.

I've been selling during most of the time I was on my school Basketball team, Volleyball team, and Track team. I was in Choir and participated in several school plays and productions. All while maintaining a 4.0 GPA. As you can imagine, I was always busy running from one place to another. But believe me when I say you can do it.

Health And Mental Benefits Of Selling

There are other benefits that selling can give you as well. Selling can bring physical benefits such as getting in exercise, stimulating brain function, release endorphins that can make you happy, help your sleep cycle, strengthen muscles, and increase your energy levels.

Selling can also give some emotional and social benefits such as resilience, which can come in handy when facing rejections while selling or doing other things. It can also help develop discipline from setting a time to focus on one specific thing or good manners from engaging in social interaction with strangers.

So, selling isn't just a waste of time to get what you want, but it's a way to prepare for the outside world with discipline, work ethic, determination, and good manners. With these traits, you can be sure to succeed in any field you choose.

Chapter One Questions

1) What are your thoughts about selling?

2) How do you think selling can affect the quality of your life?

3) What are some "unproductive tasks" you could try to eliminate?

4) How can you balance your work-school life?

CHAPTER 2: WHY GOALS ARE SO IMPORTANT

"People with clear, written goals accomplish far more in a shorter period of time than people without them could ever imagine."

-BRIAN TRACY

Okay, so you've read the benefits of selling, and you're ready to get started. Great! The question is, how do you start? The first thing you will need to do is to set a Goal.

So, let's first look and see what the definition of a goal is.

A goal, as defined by Merriam-Webster, is "the end toward which effort is directed."

In this case, an "end" would be what your desired outcome or target is. The "effort" would be the work that you do to get that desired result.

When you have a goal that you want to meet, you ultimately wish to attain success. Success can come in various forms, but the basic definition is accomplishing an aim or purpose. If you were to ask yourself what you want to succeed at in life or what goal you want to achieve, can you answer?

To make the idea of goals more comfortable for you, I want to talk about soccer for a second. What are the player's reasons for playing? Do they want to run around kicking a ball for an hour? No! The main reason for kicking the ball is to get the ball in the net, to score a goal.

Why Are Goals Important

If you don't have a goal, you will go through the motions of life, like getting a college degree, but then you end up working at a McDonald's. This happens because you earned the degree, but you didn't have any plans of what to do with it.

I know this will sound harsh, but you need to hear it. Life with no goal will leave you unhappy. A goal will give you something to work towards, a sense of direction. It can also keep you motivated to keep selling and not give up. So, now that you know why you need a goal. I will tell you five simple steps to creating one.

The 5 Steps To Creating A Goal

1. Figure out something that you want or need (Do you want to go on vacation? Purchase a car? Something else?)
2. Write down your goal(s) and the amount of time you're giving yourself.
3. Set a daily target of what you need to do to reach your goal(s).
4. Imagine yourself accomplishing your goal and keep reminding yourself of it. If you can, it is better to write it down daily.
5. Tell someone about your goal because it's much easier to have someone rooting for you.

Congratulations! You will now be on your way to accomplishing your goal. Now you can continue to achieve your other goals with this same energy.

Example Of Creating A Goal With The 5 Steps

1. I want to save up to $2,000 to buy my first car. It's a 2004 Honda Accord!!
2. I want to save $2,000 for my car in just one month. Today is January 3rd, and by February 3rd, I will have the $2,000 to pay for my Honda Accord.
3. I need to make at least $65 per day. ($2,000 divided by 31 days equals $65 a day.)
4. The day I buy my car I'm going to bring it to my best friend Brian's house, he's going to wig out. It will be so worth it!!!
5. Me: *Hey Mom, I've decided that I'm going to sell and make $2,000 to buy a 2004 Honda Accord!!!!!* Mom: *Okay, honey, you can do this!!!!*

Yes! I got my first car, and it was so worth it. Brian and all of our friends love not having to ask our parents for rides anymore!!!!

What Happens After You Set Your Goal?

So that was an example of how to set your goal and basically how it should look. Now, we're going to talk a little about what happens after you set your goal.

The most valuable part of setting that goal is that it can get you Hyper-focused and motivated on what you're doing. When you have that goal in mind, and as you get closer to it, it just feels terrific knowing that you're on that path to success. You'll get more excited! Once you've had a couple of small victories, you'll understand what I mean.

Here are two examples of some of my experiences with and without goals.

> (1) I just wanted to make some money, but I didn't have a specific amount in mind. I was selling the products that I would usually sell. I ended up spending 4 hours selling and only made $20. It's because my heart just wasn't in it. I only asked customers with half the effort that I would typically do. Complete transparency here, this would happen a lot of times when I didn't have a goal.

> (2) However, to contrast this. Here is what I accomplished with a goal. I decided on a Friday that I wanted to go to Universal Studios. My parents said that if I wanted to go,

then I would have to raise the money for mine and my brothers' tickets. I said, "No Problem." I went and hit the ground running and ended up making $500 in just two days. I ended up making enough to buy annual passes for my brother and me. Plus, I had spending cash as well.

The difference here is that in the second scenario, I had a goal that I really wanted to achieve. When I was out selling, I asked every customer "for the sale." I was hungry and eager to hit my goal. I was committed to hitting my goal. In all honesty, it didn't take much longer to make the $500 as it did the $20.

How Your Goals Will Change After You Start Selling

I like and recommend the idea of starting with a few smaller goals before moving on to bigger ones. When you do it this way, I think it can help build up your motivation. It allows you time to get better at selling while you easily knock out some smaller goals. Then, once you have some experience, you'll realize how easy it is to go out and get your money, and then you can start setting some larger goals.

Your goals will also change as you grow older. In the beginning, my goals were related to entertainment and vacations. But as time passed, they became directed towards my education. I started fundraising money for my school sports and even my tuition when I was in private school. Nowadays, I have been saving money for college. I am trying not to have to work in college so that I can stay focused on school. I am investing the time now and saving money, so I can use my time later for what is most important to me.

Don't be worried about the goals you are going to set. If they are right or not. Just set them. This is the most crucial step for you to complete. As you can tell by my previous examples, if you don't have a set goal and you try to go out to make some money, you will not get very far. So, eliminate the excuses and write down your goals right now.

Chapter 2 Questions

1) Write down the first three goals that come to your mind? Write them quickly.

1.

2.

3.

2) If you achieve these goals, how can they change your life?

3) Now write down four more goals that you would like to accomplish over the next 12 months.

1.

2.

3.

4.

CHAPTER 3: ATTITUDE IS KEY

"Remember that a product can be shopped, but a great attitude cannot. A price can be beat, but a great attitude is priceless. There's nothing more valuable to anyone than a positive person."

– GRANT CARDONE

This quote from Grant Cardone is the best description of why attitude is so important. From my own experiences, I can tell you that people are willing to spend more money on what you are selling if you have a great attitude. You must "WOW" them with a positive, can-do attitude!

Like I had said earlier, I was not always motivated and sometimes didn't have the attitude that I needed to have. One of the ways that I was able to get the right mindset was to use goals.

Goals can help change your attitude dramatically. However, only having them isn't always enough. We are going to cover a few ways that you can improve your attitude.

Always Act With A Purpose

When you have that goal in mind, make it your singular focus, just like when I wanted to raise the money to go to Universal Studios. I committed to the plan, and everything action I took was to achieve that goal.

Stretch Yourself Past Your Limits Every Day

The only limits that you have are what you place on yourself. If you think you can only make so much money in an hour, then that's what you will do. However, if you believe that there is No Limit to what you can make, it will allow you to make more than you ever imagined. So, I challenge you, set your goal for the day, and then try to double that goal in sales!

Take Action Without Expecting Results

Part of having a great attitude is having gratitude. Everything you do will not always have the result that you desire. You need to be grateful that you have the opportunity that is before you. Being grateful is especially important when selling because you will have many customers that will say "no." You need to be thankful that you had the opportunity to speak with them and then move on to ask the next customer.

Use Setbacks To Improve Your Skills

Tying directly into the previous one, hearing "no" from the customer is now your best opportunity to try to figure out why they said "no." Ask yourself, was it the way I asked? Was it the look that was on my face? Did I look angry or upset? Did I have a great attitude? Is it the product that I'm selling? You need to look at any potential reasons and try to figure out how you can overcome this next time. How could you have done it better?

Seek Out Those Who Share Your Positive Attitude

Grant Cardone always says, "you are a product of your environment." What this means is if you hang out with negative people, you're going to be negative. Just like if you were to hang out with people who do bad things, you'd probably end up doing bad things as well. The same goes for the flip side. If you hang out with positive people, you'll most likely end up reflecting that positivity in your personality. You will need to be ready to cut the negative activities out of your life or reduce the time you spend doing them.

Don't Take Yourself So Seriously

For some people, this might be easy to do, but it may be more difficult for others. What you need to do is try just to have some fun while you're selling. Don't let yourself get stressed or even angry about things. Don't take things personally. Just roll with the punches. Let yourself enjoy the moment.

Forgive The Limitations Of Others

The limitations of others can come in many different forms. The one I've encountered the most is when people see a 16-year-old out selling or fundraising money for a goal, and they give you dirty looks or just straight out say they disapprove of it. Believe it or not, some people out there don't like seeing someone being independent and trying to make things better for themselves. In these cases, you need to remember that something may have happened in their lives that caused them to think this way, maybe they weren't taught the same values that you and I were as a child, and you just need to forgive them.

Say "Thank You" More Frequently

Saying thank you is probably one of the best things you could do to develop a positive attitude. It's called the power of thank you. I honestly recommend practicing in front of the mirror. Just stand there and say thank you, and then say thank you again, and just look to see what the expression is on your face as you say it. People can feel a sincere thank you. If you tell them "thank you" and don't mean it, they'll probably notice. But if you can practice while looking in the mirror, maybe you can figure out what's the best way that you could say thank you and show them that you sincerely mean it.

Chapter Three Questions

1) What are four tips for improving your attitude?

1.

2.

3.

4.

2) Why is a great attitude priceless?

3) What does it mean to be a product of your environment?

CHAPTER 4: WHAT PRODUCT TO SELL

"A great attitude is worth more than a great product."

– GRANT CARDONE

Do you have that goal in your mind now? Yes, okay, great! Do you have the right attitude? Yes, that's fantastic! Now let's talk about what product to sell. With everything available to choose from, how do you decide what it is that you're going to sell? I think this is what people feel is the most challenging part; choosing what to sell. However, it shouldn't be. It's easy, sell a-n-y-t-h-i-n-g!

I Have Sold A Lot Of Products

Over the years, I have sold many different types of products. I have sold fundraising chocolates, fundraiser cakes and popcorn, chips, cookies, candy bars, candy apples, cotton candy, water, soda, sports drinks, and much more.

Edible Items Are Great Sellers

As you can see from my selling history, you can sell many items, but I would start with more edible items, such as chips, candy, or drinks. These items are great because people purchase them from you, eat them, and then a little later want more.

Here is a list of some edible items to get you started:

- Assorted chips such as Cheetos, Funyuns, Doritos, Lays
- Canned sodas like Coke, Dr. Pepper, Diet Coke, Sprite
- Sports Drinks such as Gatorade, Powerade, Bai, Body Armor
- Energy drinks such as Monster, Red Bull
- Candy like M&M's, Snickers, 3 Musketeers, Reese's Pieces
- Sunflower seeds, Pumpkin seeds
- Peanuts, Almonds, Pistachios
- Popcorn, Candy Coated Popcorn
- Cookies like Oreos, Chocolate Chip, Chocolate Mint
- Trail mix, Chex Mix

These are just some suggestions to get you started. I recommend that you take a walk down the aisles of your local stores and see what types of items they have to get more ideas.

Holidays Are Great For Selling

Something to also consider is what season it is. Is it summer, winter, Christmas, Valentine's Day? Every season or holiday usually has specific products created for it. So as an example, if it's Easter, you should go to a place like Dollar Tree and purchase some of their Easter candy and resell it. The same goes for Christmas or especially Halloween. Using this strategy, you can generate some significant income during these days and times.

Non-Edible Items Can Sell Well Too

Now of course edible items aren't the only things you can sell. Non-edible items can also be very good sellers. Again, depending on the holiday or season you can sell many different types of items.

Here's a list of non-edible items to think about too:

- Books, Comics
- T-shirts, Face Masks
- Bracelets, Rings, Necklaces
- Arts & Crafts
- Car Air Fresheners
- Wiper Blades
- Toys, Stuffed Animals
- Video Games, Gaming Systems
- Used or Unwanted Clothing

Again, these are just a few ideas to get you started. I would recommend making a list of everything you can think of and seeing what looks like the best bet.

Where Can I Find Products To Sell

This might seem a little intimidating at first. But it's really not. You can find products to sell at just about any store.

Here's a list of a few places I would suggest.

- Dollar Tree, The 99 Cent Store, Family Dollar, Dollar General
- Walmart, Target
- Sam's Club, Costco
- CVS, Walgreens, Rite-Aid
- Micheals, Hobby Lobby
- Any grocery store
- eBay, Amazon

As you can see, there are quite a few places to choose from. A lot of it will just depend on what type of item you're going to be selling. As I recommended a few times, we really suggest starting with edible items. These types of items sell very easily and don't require a lot of money to purchase.

Are There Any Items I Should Avoid

Well obviously, I would not recommend selling anything that is illegal to sell. You should always check and make sure the item doesn't have any legal restrictions on its sales.

Second, I also usually try to stay away from hot food items. Items like tamales, tacos, churros, basically any kind of food item that you would have to prepare yourself. I don't like to sell these items because I would hate to not properly cook something and someone gets sick because of that. If I sell a food item, it's always something that is closed and sealed by the manufacturer.

Side note about hot food items. I do see people that sell hot food items every day. This is actually a pretty popular type of item to sell. So, if you have the appropriate environment to prepare these types of items, they can be very big sellers.

Okay, having these items to sell is great, but just before you go jumping around. Do you know where to sell? No? Let me tell you!!

Chapter Four Questions

Time for some brainstorming. List as many potential products that you can sell here. Then write down where you can buy them.

CHAPTER 5: WHERE AND WHEN TO SELL

"You can sell in the day or night, it doesn't matter!!! You just need determination and motivation, and you will succeed!!!"

– TANYA ROGERS

Now that you understand where you can find items to sell, and have some ideas what to sell, we are going to talk a little bit about where to sell. Now, this isn't necessarily a science. But there are a couple of things you may want to look at when selecting a place to sell.

What Should I Look For

The first thing to look at will be the amount of traffic a location has. Basically, is it a busy place? I think it is probably pretty obvious that you want to find a location that has a lot of customers. While there is no specific number of customers I look for, I want to see the kind of place that always has cars coming in and out of the parking lot.

The second thing to look at would be if there are a lot of families shopping there. This may vary depending on what you are selling. Since I mainly sell candies and snacks, I definitely prefer that there are a lot of kids around. When they see the items I'm selling, they usually ask their parents to get something for them. Once this happens, the parents will generally buy something for everyone in the family.

Where Can I Sell

There are a lot of places that you can sell. Like I did in the chapter about where to find products to sell, I will give you a few ideas to start with, and I encourage you to think of other places.

Here are a few to start with:

- Local Grocery Stores like Ralph's, Stater Bros, Albertsons, Kroger
- Walmart, Sam's Club, Costco
- Home Depot, Lowes
- In front of local movie theaters
- Outside of Swap Meets or flea markets
- Shopping Malls, busy shopping centers
- Dollar Tree, 99 Cent Stores, Family Dollar, Dollar General stores
- Local parks, lakes, fishing areas

- Banks, Credit Unions

What Does No Solicitation Mean?

Now, something to keep in mind is that a lot of places may have rules about *No Solicitation*. No solicitation means you aren't allowed to sell there, but it doesn't mean they won't let you. I'd recommend that you find the property manager, store manager, or even the security officer of the place you want to sell and ask them for permission. I have found that a lot of times, they will let you if you just ask.

Places To Sell Used And Non-Edible Items Online

If you have chosen to sell non-edible or used items, here are some places where you may have luck selling these types of items.

- ThredUp: ThredUp is a large thrift store online. You sell your used clothes and get paid a percentage of the profit.
  More information at https://www.thredup.com/cleanout
- Tradesy: This is another thrift and consignment store online. The idea is similar to ThredUp, but Tradesy allows you to sell designer brands for lower prices, and you still get a percentage of the makings.
  More info at https://www.tradesy.com
- VarageSale: This is essentially another thrift and consignment store, but there is more freedom with the items you can sell. You can sell miscellaneous items, such as clothes, toys, furniture, or kitchenware.

More information at https://www.varagesale.com
- eBay: eBay is a widely known online space for selling all kinds of items at any value, such as electronics, shoes, clothes, phones, vintage items, and more.
  More information at https://www.ebay.com
- Instagram: This platform is a social media one mostly used for entertainment with known friends or strangers, but when used right, you can reach out and sell your items.
- Craigslist: Like eBay, this website allows you to post many items, and you can get ALL the profit.
  More info at https://losangeles.craigslist.org

Yard Sales

Another local way to sell anything is with a yard sale. Depending on your city, county, or state's rules, it is a relatively inexpensive and straightforward way to sell items. All you need to do is to get a permit, permission from your parents, and things to sell. Then you're all set.

When To Sell

Now that we've talked about where to sell, let's look at what is possibly the most crucial question, **When to Sell?** To answer this question, you simply need to ask yourself, when are your customers going to be available to buy your items?

I've personally got one rule to help guide me, "work while others play." Do you know what I'm doing on a Friday or Saturday night? I'm out in front of a movie theater or shopping mall hustling! I've made $150 in two hours in front of a movie theater on a Saturday night before. So, it's a matter of selling while others play.

Now, this may not sound great to you, but you have to think like a business owner. If you're going to have any success, you will need to make some sacrifices. This is where having goals becomes very important. If you keep thinking about the goals you want to achieve, the sacrifices become easier.

Chapter Five Questions

1) What locations do you think are the best places to sell in your city?

2) Will you have to get permission to sell at any of these places? Write them here.

3) Use this space to write down any contact information for these places.

4) What time of the day do you think will be best for you to sell?

CHAPTER 6: PRICING, INCOME, AND PROFIT

"Businesses fail, first and foremost, because their ideas weren't sold fast enough and at prices and quantities high enough to survive."

-GRANT CARDONE

This chapter will teach you how to be smart with your inventory and pricing because making money matters. There are three main parts in this chapter; pricing, income, and profit. We will be going into detail for each one.

When you sell candy bars for school fundraisers, you usually sell them for a dollar, right? Yes, but that shouldn't be the case now. You are on your way to becoming an Entrepreneur, and a dollar won't cut it anymore.

When you sell for yourself, there are lots of items to take into account. How much product do you have? How much does it cost? How much gas will it take to get to where you're selling? What are other businesses charging for the same product? So, how much will you sell it for yourself?

These are all essential questions, and it's time for you to figure out your pricing. Since I've had experience with competition in sales, I can help you understand whether you should sell at a high or low price.

Here's The Bottom Line

If you sell items at a lower price, you will probably sell more products, but it will take twice the number of products and effort to make what you could have if you would have charged a little more.

Let's take a look at an example.

> If you sell a bag of Cheetos for $1, and you sell 20. That's great. You've made $20. But the box of Cheetos you just bought was $15, so in reality, you only have $5 to spend for yourself (your profit).

Now let's make one little adjustment.

> If you sell your bag of Cheetos for $2 and you sell 20, you

now have $40, then subtract the box's cost, which was $15. That's $25 left to spend for yourself or save up.

As you can see, there can be a big difference just by making a small change to the price. The biggest takeaway here is that there is no set formula for pricing. You will need to test out different prices for the items you are selling. Don't be afraid of trying a higher price. I know it can be done.

Multiply, Don't Add

Now even though there isn't a set formula for pricing, if there was one, this would be it. In this next section, we're going to talk about what I call "multiply, don't add". What does this mean? Simply put, it means we want to multiply our money and not just add it.

Let's look at another example.

> Let's say you purchase 10 items to sell, and they cost $1 each, so your total cost is $10. Then you resell those items for $1.50 each. If you sell them all you will have made $15, leaving you with a profit of $5. Now in my world of selling, this would be an unacceptable amount of profit. I need to at least double my profit or more. The way I would price this item would be that I would resell it for at least two or three dollars.

You see, the idea here is that you need to make enough profit to be able to reinvest into your business, plus you would need money to save for your goal.

The way this scenario would work out for me is that I would purchase 10 items for $1 each, my total cost would be $10. I would then resell these items for $3 each and I would make a $30 total income. That would give me the $10 that I originally paid for the items, and it would leave me with $20 in profit to reinvest or save.

As you can tell just a little change in price can be the difference between making $5 or $20. And the worst part is that they both require the same amount of work to do. As you start to become an entrepreneur you will see how a lot of little things can make a big difference in the end.

Treat Your Product With Care

One last thought about products and pricing. You have to remember that these are items that you're going to be selling to customers. So, you must treat and handle the product with care. The way your product looks and the way it's presented will make a huge difference with being able to sell something for $1.50 versus $3.

You also need to think about what kind of product it is and where you're keeping it. So, as an example, if you're selling chocolate candy bars and it's the middle of summer, don't leave them sitting in the trunk or the back of the car because they will melt.

Income

We mentioned income in the above examples for pricing. But let's dig a little more into it.

First, let's look at the definition of Income from Investopedia:

> **Income** is money (or some equivalent value) that an individual or business receives, usually in exchange for providing a good or service.

This definition is honestly a pretty good one. Income is the money that you receive from selling products to customers. This money you receive can also be called Top Line Sales, and it means that it's the money you make before paying for the products you are selling and any other expenses.

Let's look at a simple example of income.

> You sell 10 bags of Doritos for $3.00 each
> Your total income is $30.00

That's it. As you can see from this example, Income doesn't include anything other than what you made from selling your products.

Profit

Now let's look at Profit. Here's the definition from Google:

> **Profit** is a financial gain, especially the difference between the amount earned and the amount spent buying, operating, or producing something.

This definition was the most straightforward one I could find, and it's not bad. Simply put, after you paid all your expenses, it is the money that is leftover. Like I mentioned earlier, there can be a few things you need to pay for. A couple of examples are product cost and fuel expenses. As you start selling, you should list the different things you need to pay to accurately figure out your profit.

Here's a simple example of profit.

> An item costs you $1.00
> You sell it for $3.00
> Your profit is $2.00

And it's as simple as that. You can determine your profit by subtracting your product costs from your income.

Now that you have money, what will you do with it? Spend it? Save it? Give it to your parents? ALL of those are possible, but I recommend saving it. You know why? Because once it's gone, it's gone. You don't want to spend it on selfish things. You want to spend the money when you really need something because it will help you with spending habits and money management in the long run. Save it. Really.

Chapter Six Questions

1) What is the importance of selling your product at a little higher price?

2) Have you thought about what price you want to sell your products for?

3) Why do you think presentation matters?

4) Can you explain the difference between income and profit?

CHAPTER 7: HOW TO SELL

"If you are not willing to learn, no one can help you. If you are determined to learn, no one can stop you."

-ZIG ZIGLAR

We're almost at the end, and I want to congratulate you because you've read this book. Now I will give you some last-minute training to truly succeed in sales.

The first part I want to talk about is the thoughts and actions that are required to do the type of selling that we're doing.

Attitude is the basis of everything you do. Without having the right attitude, you will not be able to achieve any of your goals. Attitude alone can make or break your chances of success.

Understanding is an essential part of how we think and speak with our customers. Remember how we spoke about the fact that 76% of Americans are living paycheck to paycheck, this also includes our customers. They may want to help us by making a purchase but simply cannot spare any money to do so right now. So when your customer says no to you, have compassion and try to understand where they're coming from.

Sincerity is something that your customers can feel from you. When you are asking them to make a purchase from you and explaining what it's for, they will have a feeling inside of whether you are being sincere. This is why you must always be sincere and honest with your customers when you ask them for *the sale*. It's good to let your customers know that the reason you are selling is that you want to do something or go somewhere. If they know what your goal is they may be more willing to help.

Passion is something *you* must feel. If you have written your goals and truly want to achieve them, you need to be passionate about what you are doing. Your customers should be able to feel your passion when you're speaking to them. If your customer can feel this passion from you, they will be a lot more willing to help you reach those goals.

Speed is a key ingredient to the type of sales we are doing. We are catching our customers off guard as they are going to or leaving a place. This is a place where they did not expect to have someone like us asking them to make a purchase. A lot of times our customers may be in the middle of something and are in a rush, because of this we need to make sure that we are speedy and efficient when we ask them for the sale. However, this is not a reason to be rude to a customer. Just be quick and efficient.

The Sales Process

So, we have boiled our sales process down to 5 simple steps. These are similar to other sales processes and can be used for most types of businesses you may start. Let me briefly explain each step.

Step 1: Greet the customer

As we mentioned earlier, our customers are not expecting us to interrupt their day. So, we must make our greeting very quick and simple. You should say something like "good morning sir/ma'am" or "hello, may I have a quick moment of your time?"

Step 2: Build value

In this next step, the way we are going to build value for our customers is to let them know why we are selling these items. This is where you'll tell them about what you're trying to achieve and what the money is going to do.

For example, if I was raising money to go on a field trip for school, I would say something like this: *May I ask for your help. I am raising money to go on my school field trip to Washington D.C. I need to raise $1000 in* *the next three weeks, would you be able to help me reach my goal?*

Step 3: Offer choices

After you have built value by stating what your goals are, your next step will be to offer your customer the choices of what products you have available. This is where you'll tell them what items you have and how much they cost.

Step 4: Ask for the sale

In this step, you are now going to simply ask them what items they would like to purchase. As an example, you could say something like "which item would you like today?" or "which item would you like to support me with today?"

Step 5: Close the sale

In the "close the sale" step all we mean is accepting payment from the customer and telling them "thank you for their support."

If you follow these steps with every customer you interact with, your chances of making a sale will increase. Especially after you have been doing this for a while, it will start to come to you easily and naturally.

Training Time

The last thing I want to cover with you is some example scenarios you may encounter with customers.

SCENARIO 1: Example of a customer SALE

> You: *Hello, good afternoon, sir/ma'am. Can I take up a moment of your time?*
>
> Customer: *No, thank you.*
>
> You: *I'm sorry, but it will only take a moment.*
>
> Customer: *Fine. Hurry up. I'm in a rush.*
>
> You: *Of course, sir/ma'am, I'm fundraising money for _____ and I am selling these items for _____ (price.) Would you like to support me?*
>
> Customer: *Very well. I'll take one of ____, and you can keep the change.*
>
> You: *Thank you so much, sir/ma'am, have a great day!*

This is an example of a sale where the customer wasn't necessarily in the best mood, but your positive and humble attitude changed that, and you made a certain amount of money.

Do be careful. If the customer looks too angry or is on the phone, I wouldn't ask them then. Maybe wait for them to come back out from where they are going. Always read body language.

SCENARIO 2: Example of customer REJECTION

> You: *Good morning, sir/ma'am, I'm selling these items to go (here), and I'm asking if you could be so kind as to make a purchase?*
>
> Customer: *Well, how much do they cost?*

> You: *Well, this is ____, and these are _____.*
>
> Customer: *Oh no, these are too expensive.*
>
> You: *Yes, I understand, ma'am/sir. But if you could maybe support my cause with a donation?*
>
> Customer: *No, I'm sorry. I don't have any money to give.*
>
> You: *No problem, have a great day!*

Okay, so what happened here was the customer was nice, but didn't want to spend too much money on your product. And that is completely okay because there will always be rejections. You need to learn to take these and stay positive. Don't throw an attitude at them because it will only make it worse. Keep a good reputation. Don't be afraid to change up your greeting or ending too. It can get boring saying the same thing over and over again.

These are just two scenarios, fairly typical, and at a later time, more can be written in a mini book dedicated to this subject. But for now, whatever happens, stay positive and never give up 3 feet from success.

Chapter Seven Questions

1) Use this blank space to write down any rejections you get from customers and how you think you should respond.

CHAPTER 8: PUTTING THE PIECES TOGETHER

"Knowing information is not the same as owning it and following through. Information without execution is poverty."

-TONY ROBBINS

Right now is the best opportunity for you to achieve success. You have read about the different parts of this process I used to create $4,000 of income in just two months. Master these following parts so that you can do the same. Let's recap these parts and see how they all work together.

Goals

It all starts with having that goal. Like I said earlier, if you don't have a goal that you're working towards, it can impact how well you do. It's like running in a race and not knowing where the finish line is. You need to know where the end is so that it can give you that extra burst of energy and motivation to push past it.

Attitude

If you don't have the right attitude, you will never be able to have success. You need to use your goals to help fuel your motivation and give you a positive can-do attitude. You need to cut out any negative activities and only focus on things that will make you a more positive person. Remember that a customer will pay more for a positive attitude than they will for a product.

Product

Once you have set your goals and got your attitude in the right place, you will need to decide on a product or two to sell. You will probably need to experiment with some different products to find out what works best in your area. You can find a product to sell just about anywhere. One tip when you do, look to see what the store runs out of the most or what always has low stock. An item that is usually low or out of stock could indicate that the product is popular in your area.

Where To Sell

Now that you have the goals, attitude, and product. You need to commit to going out and selling it. Just a reminder, you can't make money without going out and asking for it. Find a location that is busy with customers. Grocery stores, Warehouse stores, Dollar Stores are all excellent places to sell. Remember that you may need to ask for permission to sell from the management. So, make sure to find out.

When To Sell

You have all the skills, but now you need to plan when you're going to do this.

I want to say first, know why you're selling and state that in your head.

Second, know how much time you want to contribute to this goal and when your customers will be out there to buy from you.

If your goal is to go to a field trip in a week and it's $40, plus $40 for spending money, that's $80 divided by seven days, which is approximately 12 dollars a day. Now, that's not so hard, maybe 1 hour a day in the beginning to half an hour a day later with more experience. Also, understand that bigger goals=more time, so don't expect to make a ton of money your first day. Be patient.

Pricing

Having the right price can be crucial to you achieving your goal in less time. You do not want to underprice your products. At the same time, you do not want to rip off people either. Be fair when considering your prices. Remember, the goal is to make enough profit that you can achieve your goals. If you tell your customers what the purchase is for, they will usually love to help you achieve it, especially if you have a great attitude.

Income

The total sales that you have made before paying for your expenses are your income. Be careful not to confuse this money with your profit.

Profit

It is everything you have after paying all your expenses. You can put this money towards your goal. Also, you can use some of it to re-invest in more products. After all, to keep making more money, you will need more products to sell.

Training

We covered a couple of common scenarios in this book. However, you will have many different situations that will come up. You will need to keep these in your head and try to figure out how you can overcome these objections. I recommend practicing different responses or reactions to these until you are comfortable addressing it when a customer says them to you. Remember also to stay positive. Don't let them get you down.

The Sum Of All The Parts

Once you master all these different parts, you will have no problem generating income when you need it. After I had gotten all these pieces working together, I had no trouble making $4,000 in 60 days. In all honesty, I haven't had any difficulty duplicating it even today.

Call To Action

Here is your Call to Action! Go out and purchase your products and **START SELLING!** Don't Delay! Take Action and Take Action Now!

Here is where I cut the cord. Congratulations again for taking this step to success, and I wish you the best of luck in your future!!!!

Chapter Eight Questions

1) Do you understand how these parts all work together?

2) Do you believe that you can duplicate these yourself to make $4,000 in two months?

3) Is there any particular topic that you believe you need to learn more about?

SIGN UP FOR THE SELLING FOR KIDS NEWSLETTER

Stay up to date on our New Releases, Deals and More by signing up to our mailing list!

Sign Up Here >> SellingForKids.com

When you sign up for our Selling for Kids newsletter. We give you access to exclusive deals and offers, Advance Reader copies of our books, plus lots of tips, tricks and training to help you on your journey into entrepreneurship.

ABOUT THE AUTHOR

Tanya Rogers

Tanya Rogers is a 16-year-old author, entrepreneur, blogger, content creator, podcaster, and high school senior. Along with her family, Tanya has dedicated their time to creating the Selling for Kids Book Series to inspire and teach future young entrepreneurs how to start their own business. Their primary focus has been teaching an easy and inexpensive method for kids and teens to start their first business.

She's also created two blogs for education and finance. She also runs a podcast where she talks about business-related topics and tips to achieve mental health. Plus, she's co-writer with other authors on the Chang'E Project, a non-profit feminist organization dedicated to breaking down gender-based stigmas and improve women's education.

ABOUT THE AUTHOR

David Rogers

David Rogers is an entrepreneur, author, trainer, and public speaker. David has been in sales for almost 30 years and dedicates a lot of his time to training.

Along with his daughter, Tanya, and son Ethan, David has dedicated his time to creating the Selling for Kids Book Series to inspire and teach future young entrepreneurs how they can start their own business. Their primary focus has been teaching an easy and inexpensive method for kids and teens to start their first business.

BOOKS IN THIS SERIES

SELLING FOR KIDS BOOK SERIES

Selling for Kids The Book Series was created to help teach and inspire a future generation of young entrepreneurs.

The Kids Guide To Selling: How I Was Able To Make $4,000 In 60 Days

In our first book, The Kids Guide to Selling, we teach you about the nine fundamental principles you need to know to start your first business. Plus, you learn what you need to do Right Now to start selling and generating an income, following our simple and inexpensive business model.

The Teens Guide To Starting Your Own Business: Your Step By Step Blueprint To Becoming A Teen Entrepreneur

In our second book, The Teens Guide to Starting Your Own Business, we dig even deeper into the concepts of starting your own business and becoming a teen entrepreneur. Plus, we give you the step-by-step Blueprint of what, when, and how you need to do to launch your first business successfully.

The Teens Guide To Becoming An Entrepreneur: 102 Ways That You Can Start To Think Like A Successful Entrepreneur

In our third book, we will take your knowledge and skills to the next level by introducing you to the idea of creating the Entrepreneur's Mindset. We will be showing you 102 ways that you can start to think like a successful entrepreneur.

The Teens Guide To Mastering Sales: How You Need To Think To Become Successful At Selling

In the Teens Guide to Mastering Sales, we will show you how you need to think to become a master at selling. Your ability to sell, persuade, or convince others is a critical key to having success in business or life.

FOLLOW US

You Can Stay Up To Date

Instagram: instagram.com/sellingforkids

Facebook: facebook.com/sellingforkids

Amazon (Tanya): amazon.com/author/tanyarogers

Amazon (David): amazon.com/author/daverogers

Website: sellingforkids.com

www.ingramcontent.com/pod-product-compliance
Lightning Source LLC
Chambersburg PA
CBHW031544210526
45464CB00003B/1148